How to Solve Wor...

Word problems can be short math stories or sentences that give number facts. Word problems usually end in a question. You use math to answer the question or solve the problem.

Read

Read the word problem: Make a picture in your mind about what you read.

Ask yourself: What is the word problem about?

Think

Read the problem again: Think about the facts or details.

Ask yourself: What do I need to find out?

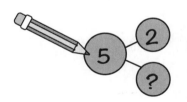

Draw

Draw a picture of the problem: Draw a part for each number. Draw a part for the number you are trying to find.

Ask yourself: What does each number mean?

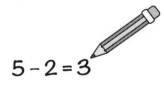

5 – 2 = 3

Solve

Solve the problem: Decide what to do with the numbers. Sometimes you will do more than one thing.

Ask yourself: What do I need to count, add, or subtract? Is there more than one step?

Check

Check your answer: Write your answer in your picture.

Ask yourself: Does my answer make sense?

1

Daily Word Problems

WEEK 1 • DAY 1

At the Park

Ryan and Allie went to the park. They got there at 10:00.

Ryan and Allie played at the park for 1 hour. At what time did they leave?

Work Space:

Show your answer on the clock.

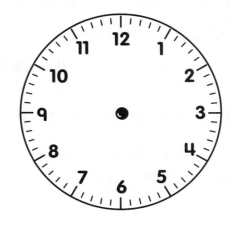

Answer:

_____ : _____

Daily Word Problems

WEEK 1 • DAY 2

At the Park

There are 12 children on the swings. Five of them are boys.

How many children are girls?

Work Space:

Answer:

_____ girls

Daily Word Problems

WEEK 1 • DAY 3

At the Park

Four children were at the slide. Ryan and Allie joined them. Then 5 more children came.

How many children were playing on the slide?

Work Space:

Answer:

_____ children

Daily Word Problems

WEEK 1 • DAY 4

At the Park

There were 6 benches at the park. Two people sat on each bench.

How many people were sitting on benches?

Work Space:

Answer:

_____ people

Daily Word Problems

At the Park

Look at the graph.

It shows how many children were at the park.

Swings	☺ ☺ ☺ ☺ ☺
Slide	☺ ☺
Sandbox	☺ ☺ ☺ ☺ ☺ ☺
Jungle Gym	☺ ☺ ☺ ☺ ☺ ☺ ☺

☺ = 1 child

1. How many more children were in the sandbox than on the slide? _____ children

2. How many more children were on the jungle gym than the swings? _____ children

Daily Word Problems

WEEK 2 • DAY 1

Cats at Play

Fluffy and Stripes are cats. They like to chase each other. They chase each other 5 times a day!

How many times do they chase each other in a week?

Work Space:

Answer:

_____ times

Daily Word Problems

WEEK 2 • DAY 2

Cats at Play

Fluffy went outside to play. She went out at 7:30 in the morning. She came back in after 1 hour.

At what time did Fluffy come back in?

Work Space:

Show your answer on the clock.

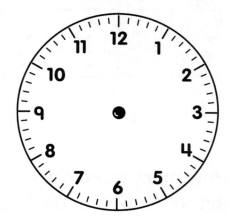

Answer:

_____:_____

Daily Word Problems

WEEK 2 • DAY 3

Cats at Play

Dylan bought a toy for his cat. The toy cost 70¢. Dylan paid with 6 dimes and some nickels.

How many nickels did he use?

Work Space:

Answer:

_____ nickels

Daily Word Problems

WEEK 2 • DAY 4

Cats at Play

There were 9 kittens playing with yarn. Three kittens were white and two were black. The rest were gray.

How many gray kittens were there?

Work Space:

Answer:

_____ kittens

Daily Word Problems

WEEK 2 • DAY 5

Cats at Play

Look at the cat.
Then fill in the missing numbers on the chart.

_____ ears

_____ eyes   _____ tail

_____ nose   _____ legs

1. How many eyes would 2 cats have?   _____ eyes

2. How many ears would 3 cats have?   _____ ears

3. How many legs would 4 cats have?   _____ legs

Daily Word Problems

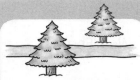

Nature Walk

WEEK 3 • DAY 1

Arissa went for a walk in the woods with her dad. They left home at 1:30. "Be back in 2 hours," said Arissa's mom.

At what time did Arissa and her dad have to be back?

Work Space:

Show your answer on the clock.

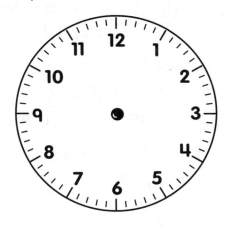

Answer:

_____:_____

Daily Word Problems

Nature Walk

WEEK 3 • DAY 2

Arissa and her dad saw 7 bunnies and 5 lizards. They also saw 3 frogs.

How many animals did they see?

Work Space:

Answer:

_____ animals

Daily Word Problems

WEEK 3 · DAY 3

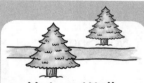

Nature Walk

There were 11 nuts on the ground. Arissa watched a squirrel take 4 of the nuts.

How many nuts were still on the ground?

Work Space:

Answer:

_____ nuts

Daily Word Problems

WEEK 3 · DAY 4

Nature Walk

Arissa saw 7 ladybugs. Each one had 2 spots.

How many spots did she see?

Work Space:

Answer:

_____ spots

Daily Word Problems

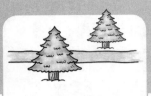

Nature Walk

Arissa picked 12 flowers on her walk. Her mom put them into two vases.

What is one way her mom could have put the flowers into the vases?

Draw the flowers in the vases. Then write a number sentence to match.

_____ + _____ = _____

Daily Word Problems

WEEK 4 • DAY 1

Pet Day

It was Pet Day at school. In Miss Tate's class, 20 students brought pets and 5 did not.

How many students were in Miss Tate's class?

Work Space:

Answer:

_____ students

Daily Word Problems

WEEK 4 • DAY 2

Pet Day

Rani brought her parrot Squawk to class. Squawk has been in Rani's family for 11 years.

Squawk was 7 when Rani's family got him. How old is Squawk now?

Work Space:

Answer:

_____ years old

Daily Word Problems

WEEK 4 • DAY 3

Pet Day

Cody brought his snake for Pet Day. When Cody first got Wiggles, the snake was 10 inches long. Now it is 30 inches long.

How much did Wiggles grow?

Work Space:

Answer:

_____ inches

Daily Word Problems

WEEK 4 • DAY 4

Pet Day

Janna brought her dog Pip to school. Use the clues to find the dog's weight.

The number is greater than 35. It is less than 45.

The number in the tens place is 3 more than the number in the ones place.

Work Space:

Answer:

Pip weighs _____ pounds.

Daily Word Problems

Pet Day

Mrs. Gill asked her class, "What kind of pets do you have?" This is what she found out.

Kind of Pet	Number of Students
Dog	8
Cat	6
Fish	3
Bird	2
Hamster	5
No Pet	4

How many more students have pets than do **not** have pets?

_____ students

Daily Word Problems

WEEK 5 • DAY 1

Piggy Bank

Shane opened his piggy bank. He took out 3 nickels and 4 dimes.

How much money did Shane take?

Work Space:

Answer:

_____ ¢

Daily Word Problems

WEEK 5 • DAY 2

Piggy Bank

Korena put 6 nickels in her piggy bank. Jamal put 10 nickels in his piggy bank.

How much more money did Jamal put in his bank than Korena?

Work Space:

Answer:

_____ ¢ more

Daily Word Problems

WEEK 5 • DAY 3

Piggy Bank

Lani has 70¢ in her piggy bank. She has only dimes and quarters. Lani has 2 quarters.

How many dimes does she have?

Work Space:

Answer:

_____ dimes

Daily Word Problems

WEEK 5 • DAY 4

Piggy Bank

Nic had 60¢ in his piggy bank. Then he put in 1 nickel and 3 pennies.

How much money does Nic have in his bank now?

Work Space:

Answer:

_____ ¢

Daily Word Problems

Piggy Bank

Clay took all of these coins out of his piggy bank.

He kept 46¢. Then he put the rest of the coins back into his bank.

Circle the coins Clay kept. How much money did he put back into his piggy bank?

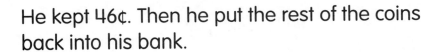

_____ ¢

Daily Word Problems

WEEK 6 • DAY 1

Toy Store

The toy store had 3 shelves of teddy bears. Each shelf had 4 bears.

How many teddy bears did the store have?

Work Space:

Write an addition sentence to solve the problem.

_____ + _____ + _____ = _____

Answer:

_____ teddy bears

Daily Word Problems

WEEK 6 • DAY 2

Toy Store

There were five toy racing cars. Each car had a number. The numbers were 53, 28, 81, 67, and 46. The cars were lined up in order from the smallest number to the largest.

What was the order of the cars?

Work Space:

Answer:

_____, _____, _____, _____, _____

Daily Word Problems • EMC 7112 • © Evan-Moor Corp.

Daily Word Problems

WEEK 6 • DAY 3

Toy Store

One whistle costs 20¢. Kai has 2 quarters.

How many whistles can Kai buy?

Work Space:

Answer:

_____ whistles

Daily Word Problems

WEEK 6 • DAY 4

Toy Store

Dana bought two sets of blocks. The first set had 32 blocks. The second set had 64 blocks.

How many blocks did Dana buy?

Work Space:

Answer:

_____ blocks

Daily Word Problems

Toy Store

Look at the chart. It shows how many toys were sold last week.

Toys Sold Last Week	
Stuffed Toys	卌 卌 卌 l
Superhero Toys	卌 卌 卌 lll
Puzzles	卌
Games	卌 卌

卌 = 5

1. How many more stuffed toys were sold than puzzles?

_____ more

2. How many more superhero toys were sold than games?

_____ more

3. How many toys were sold in all?

_____ toys

Daily Word Problems • EMC 7112 • © Evan-Moor Corp.

Daily Word Problems

At the Aquarium

Maria went to the aquarium. At the Tropical Fish Gallery, she counted 10 red fish. She also counted 20 yellow fish and 8 blue fish.

How many fish did Maria count?

Work Space:

Answer:

_____ fish

Daily Word Problems

At the Aquarium

There were 4 octopuses lying in a tank. Each octopus had 8 arms.

How many arms were there in the tank?

Work Space:

Answer:

_____ arms

Daily Word Problems

WEEK 7 • DAY 3

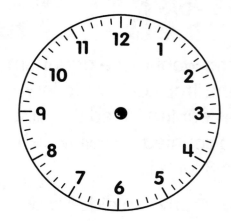

At the Aquarium

The Aqua Theater is showing a movie at 2:00. Maria's dad said, "We have half an hour before the movie starts."

What time was it?

Work Space:

Show your answer on the clock.

Answer:

_____ : _____

Daily Word Problems

WEEK 7 • DAY 4

At the Aquarium

Maria bought a pack of fish stickers at the gift shop. The pack cost 45¢. Maria paid with three coins.

What coins did Maria use?

Work Space:

Answer:

_____

_____

Daily Word Problems

WEEK 7 • DAY 5

At the Aquarium

Look at the chart. It shows the lengths of some sharks.

Mako Shark
10 feet

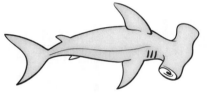

Hammerhead Shark
20 feet

Whale Shark
40 feet

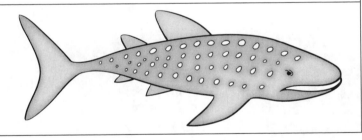

1. How much longer is the hammerhead shark than the mako shark?

_____ feet longer

2. How much longer is the whale shark than the hammerhead shark?

_____ feet longer

3. How much longer is the whale shark than the mako shark?

_____ feet longer

Daily Word Problems

WEEK 8 • DAY 1

The Bakery

Zac went to the bakery. He bought 14 banana muffins and 6 apple muffins.

How many more banana muffins did he buy than apple muffins?

Work Space:

Answer:

_____ more

Daily Word Problems

WEEK 8 • DAY 2

The Bakery

Mrs. Singh bought treats. She bought 10 date bars, 3 sweet rolls, and 5 fruit tarts.

How many treats did she buy altogether?

Work Space:

Answer:

_____ treats

Daily Word Problems

WEEK 8 • DAY 3

The Bakery

The baker made a birthday cake. He sprinkled candies all over it. He used 35 red candies and 40 yellow candies.

How many candies did the baker use on the cake?

Work Space:

Answer:

_____ candies

Daily Word Problems

WEEK 8 • DAY 4

The Bakery

Keisha will buy an even number of cookies. Use the clues to find out how many she will buy.

The number is greater than 16. It is less than 24.

You say the number when you count by fives.

Work Space:

Answer:

_____ cookies

Daily Word Problems

WEEK 8 • DAY 5

The Bakery

Look at the sign. Then answer the questions.

cookie   25¢

muffin   40¢

pie   50¢

1. Tatum has 1 dime and 3 nickels.
   What can she buy?

   _____

2. Alton bought a slice of pie. He paid
   with quarters. How many quarters
   did he use?   _____ quarters

3. Kaya bought a cookie and a muffin.
   She paid with 1 nickel and some dimes.
   How many dimes did she use?   _____ dimes

Daily Word Problems

WEEK 9 • DAY 1

Magic Show

Marvo the Magician pulled out rabbits from his hat. First he pulled out 12 white rabbits. Then he pulled out 14 gray rabbits.

How many rabbits did Marvo pull out of his hat?

Work Space:

Answer:

_____ rabbits

Daily Word Problems

WEEK 9 • DAY 2

Magic Show

Marvo put 25 eggs in his hat. Then he put in 7 more. Marvo said, "Hocus-pocus!" He turned his hat upside down. The eggs were gone!

How many eggs disappeared?

Work Space:

Answer:

_____ eggs

Daily Word Problems

WEEK 9 • DAY 3

Magic Show

Marvo held up 4 pieces of rope. Each piece was 12 inches long. Marvo said, "Presto!" The 4 pieces joined together into one long piece.

How long was the long piece of rope?

Work Space:

Answer:

_____ inches

Daily Word Problems

WEEK 9 • DAY 4

Magic Show

Marvo put his hand behind his ear. He pulled out a coin! He put the coin on a table. Marvo pulled out more coins. When he was done, he had 3 rows of coins. Each row had 2 coins.

How many coins were there?

Work Space:

Answer:

_____ coins

Daily Word Problems

Magic Show

Marvo is holding a card with a number on it. The number is on the chart. Use the clues to help you figure out the number.

1	2	3	4	5	6	7	8	9	10
11	12	13	14	15	16	17	18	19	20
21	22	23	24	25	26	27	28	29	30
31	32	33	34	35	36	37	38	39	40
41	42	43	44	45	46	47	48	49	50
51	52	53	54	55	56	57	58	59	60
61	62	63	64	65	66	67	68	69	70
71	72	73	74	75	76	77	78	79	80
81	82	83	84	85	86	87	88	89	90
91	92	93	94	95	96	97	98	99	100

Clues:
- The number is greater than 50.
- The number is less than 80.
- The sum of the digits is 14.
- The ones digit is 2 more than the tens digit.

What is the number? _____

Daily Word Problems

WEEK 10 • DAY 1

School Days

Morgan's school starts at 8:30. It takes her half an hour to walk to school.

At what time should Morgan leave home to get to school on time?

Work Space:

Show your answer on the clock.

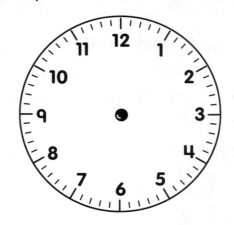

Answer:

_____ : _____

Daily Word Problems

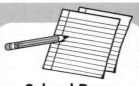

WEEK 10 • DAY 2

School Days

The science teacher cut four apples. Two apples had 10 seeds each. One apple had 8 seeds and another had 6.

How many seeds were there in the apples?

Work Space:

Answer:

_____ seeds

Daily Word Problems

WEEK 10 • DAY 3

School Days

Mr. Yee put his students' drawings on the wall.
He put them in 4 rows.
Each row had 5 pictures.

How many drawings were on the wall?

Work Space:

Answer:

_____ drawings

Daily Word Problems

WEEK 10 • DAY 4

School Days

There were 87 students in second grade. There were 75 students in first grade.

How many more students were in second grade than in first grade?

Work Space:

Answer:

_____ more students

Daily Word Problems

School Days

Five classes had a recycling contest.
The class that collected the most bottles
would win a pizza party.

Look at the chart. It shows how many bottles were collected.

Number of Bottles Collected for Recycling

Class	A	B	C	D	E
Number of Bottles	60	73	57	76	69

1. Write the numbers in order from the least to the greatest.

   _____ _____ _____ _____ _____

2. Which class won the pizza party?   Class _____

Daily Word Problems

WEEK 11 • DAY 1

Tasty Snacks

Tyson and Annie each had a box of animal crackers. Tyson's box had 41 crackers. Annie's box had 38 crackers.

How many crackers did they have altogether?

Work Space:

Answer:

_____ crackers

Daily Word Problems

WEEK 11 • DAY 2

Tasty Snacks

Mr. Popper sells popcorn. In the morning, he filled 95 bags of popcorn. By that evening, he had only 11 bags left.

How many bags of popcorn did he sell?

Work Space:

Answer:

_____ bags

Daily Word Problems

WEEK 11 • DAY 3

Tasty Snacks

Juan loves pickles. Every day he eats 2 dill pickles and 3 sweet pickles.

How many pickles would Juan eat in two weeks?

Work Space:

Answer:

_____ pickles

Daily Word Problems

Tasty Snacks

WEEK 11 • DAY 4

Maddy had a bag of pretzels. The number of pretzels was greater than 35 but less than 50. The number's tens digit was 1 more than the ones digit.

How many pretzels were in the bag?

Work Space:

Answer:

_____ pretzels

Daily Word Problems

Tasty Snacks

At Ice Cream Delight, all ice cream cones cost 1 dollar.

Ice Cream Delight
Our cones are always one dollar!

1. Vanna bought a vanilla cone.
   She paid with dimes.
   How many dimes did she use?   _____ dimes

2. Stacy bought a chocolate cone.
   She paid with quarters.
   How many quarters did she use?   _____ quarters

3. Jadan bought a strawberry cone.
   He paid with nickels.
   How many nickels did he use?   _____ nickels

Daily Word Problems

WEEK 12 • DAY 1

At the Movies

Caleb and Jake went to the movies. Each ticket cost 10 dollars. Caleb and Jake also shared a bag of popcorn. The popcorn cost 5 dollars.

How much did the tickets and popcorn cost altogether?

Work Space:

Answer:

_____ dollars

Daily Word Problems

WEEK 12 • DAY 2

At the Movies

There were 38 people waiting in line to see <u>Dinosaurs from Space</u>. Then 7 more people came.

How many people were waiting in line to see the movie?

Work Space:

Answer:

_____ people

Daily Word Problems

WEEK 12 • DAY 3

At the Movies

The dinosaur movie started 2 hours ago. It is now 2:30.

At what time did the movie start?

Work Space:

Show your answer on the clock.

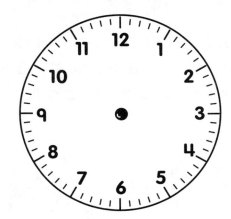

Answer:

_____ : _____

Daily Word Problems

WEEK 12 • DAY 4

At the Movies

Mia bought some mints before the movie started. The mints cost 50¢. Mia paid with some coins.

What coins could Mia have used? How many did she use of each?

Work Space:

Draw the coins.

Answer:

_____

_____

At the Movies

Mrs. Cortez asked her students, "What kind of movies do you like best?" She made a graph to show what she found out.

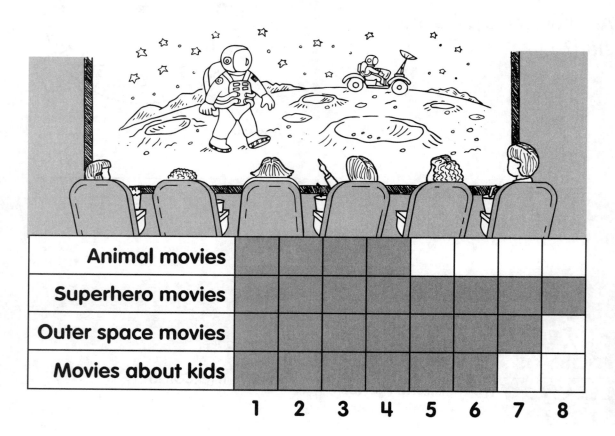

	1	2	3	4	5	6	7	8
Animal movies								
Superhero movies								
Outer space movies								
Movies about kids								

1. What kind of movie did most students like the best?

   _____

2. What kind of movie was the least popular?

   _____

3. How many more students liked movies about kids than movies about animals?

   _____ more students

Daily Word Problems

WEEK 13 • DAY 1

Zing's Planet

Zing lives on the planet Zong. He likes to zip around in his spaceship.

Zing travels 100 miles an hour. How many miles does he travel in 4 hours?

Work Space:

Count by 100 to solve the problem. Fill in the missing numbers.

100, _____, _____, _____

Answer:

_____ miles

Daily Word Problems

WEEK 13 • DAY 2

Zing's Planet

Zing's planet has many kinds of bugs. Zing likes the Ick the best. The Ick has 23 red feet and 41 yellow feet.

How many feet does the Ick have altogether?

Work Space:

Answer:

_____ feet

Daily Word Problems

WEEK 13 • DAY 3

Zing's Planet

The flowers on Zing's planet have curly petals. Each flower has 85 petals. Thirty petals have stripes. The rest have spots.

How many petals have spots?

Work Space:

Answer:

_____ petals

Daily Word Problems

WEEK 13 • DAY 4

Zing's Planet

The planet Zong has huge caves that glow in the dark. Zing has explored 48 of them. He still has 9 more to explore.

How many caves are on the planet?

Work Space:

Answer:

_____ caves

Daily Word Problems

WEEK 13 · DAY 5

Zing's Planet

The planet Zong has three moons. Each moon has large holes called craters. The holes are shaped like the numbers 5, 3, and 7.

Every night the moons line up in a row and form a 3-digit number.

1. What is the largest number that the moons can make? _____

2. What is the smallest number that the moons can make? _____

3. Write the six different numbers that the moons can make. List them in order from the smallest to the largest.

_____ , _____ , _____ , _____ , _____ , _____

Daily Word Problems

WEEK 14 • DAY 1

At the Fair

The first 300 people at the fair got free popcorn. The next 100 got free ice cream. The next 100 got free lemonade. The next 100 got free balloons.

How many people got something free?

Work Space:

Start at 300. Count by 100 to solve the problem. Fill in the missing numbers.

300, _____, _____, _____

Answer:

_____ people

Daily Word Problems

WEEK 14 • DAY 2

At the Fair

In the morning, 100 children rode the merry-go-round. In the afternoon, 200 children rode the merry-go-round.

How many children went on the merry-go-round?

Work Space:

Answer:

_____ children

Daily Word Problems

At the Fair

WEEK 14 • DAY 3

The puppet show starts in 15 minutes. It is now 11:00.

At what time will the puppet show start?

Work Space:

Show your answer on the clock.

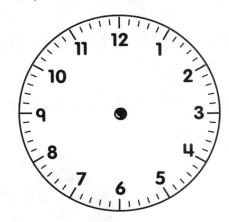

Answer:

_____ : _____

Daily Word Problems

At the Fair

WEEK 14 • DAY 4

The Click-Clack train has 15 cars. Each car can hold 2 people.

How many people can ride the train?

Work Space:

Answer:

_____ people

Daily Word Problems

At the Fair

Amber wants to buy two different toys at the fair. She has $1.00.

Amber will choose a dog, rabbit, bear, or lion.

Write the pairs Amber can pay for. Write how much money each pair would cost. One has been done for you.

dog, bear   40¢ + 50¢ = 90¢

_____

_____

_____

_____

Daily Word Problems

WEEK 15 • DAY 1

Dog Wash

Emi and her friends had a dog wash to earn money. They started washing dogs at 9:15. They took a lunch break 3 hours later.

At what time did Emi and her friends start their break?

Work Space:

Show your answer on the clock.

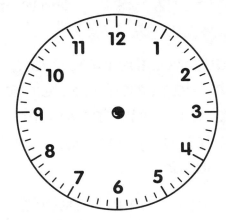

Answer:

_____ : _____

Daily Word Problems

WEEK 15 • DAY 2

Dog Wash

Emi and Sid each washed 7 dogs. Ryan and Maria each washed 6 dogs.

How many dogs did they wash in all?

Work Space:

Answer:

_____ dogs

Scruffy was the largest dog at the dog wash. He weighed 65 pounds. Muffin was the smallest dog. She weighed 14 pounds.

How many pounds heavier was Scruffy than Muffin?

Work Space:

Answer:

_____ pounds

Emi washed a poodle named Fifi. It took Emi 15 minutes to wash the dog. Emi started at 2:30.

At what time did Emi finish washing Fifi?

Work Space:

Show your answer on the clock.

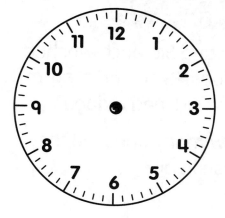

Answer:

_____ : _____

Daily Word Problems

Dog Wash

Emi and her friends made a sign for their dog wash.

The children washed 12 big dogs, 4 medium dogs, and 10 small dogs. How much money did they make?

$_____

Come to Our
Dog Wash!
Friendliest Place in Town!

Dog Size	Price
Big	$5
Medium	$4
Small	$2

Daily Word Problems

WEEK 16 • DAY 1

Under the Sea

There were 24 crabs resting on the ocean floor. Then 8 crabs crawled away.

How many crabs were still on the ocean floor?

Work Space:

Answer:

_____ crabs

Daily Word Problems

WEEK 16 • DAY 2

Under the Sea

There were 11 sea stars in the sea. Each one had 5 arms.

How many arms were there altogether?

Work Space:

Answer:

_____ arms

Daily Word Problems

WEEK 16 • DAY 3

Under the Sea

A group of 15 dolphins were swimming in the ocean. Then a group of 16 joined them.

How many dolphins were swimming together?

Work Space:

Answer:

_____ dolphins

Daily Word Problems

WEEK 16 • DAY 4

Under the Sea

There were 150 fish by a cave. Every hour, a group of 10 fish joined them.

How many fish were by the cave after 3 hours?

Work Space:

Start at 150. Count by tens to solve the problem. Fill in the missing numbers.

150, _____, _____, _____

Answer:

_____ fish

Daily Word Problems

WEEK 16 • DAY 5

Under the Sea

A diver dove deep into the sea. She kept track of the animals she saw. Later, she made a chart.

1. How many more eels were there than sea turtles?

   _____ more

2. How many more clownfish were there than octopuses?

   _____ more

Octopus	|||
Clownfish	⦀ ⦀ ⦀ ||
Eel	⦀ ⦀ ||||
Sea Turtle	⦀ ||

3. How many animals did the diver see in all?

   _____ animals

Daily Word Problems

WEEK 17 • DAY 1

Sea Horses

The Pacific sea horse is 30 centimeters long. The zebra sea horse is 8 centimeters long.

How many more centimeters long is the Pacific sea horse than the zebra sea horse?

Work Space:

Answer:

_____ centimeters

Daily Word Problems

WEEK 17 • DAY 2

Sea Horses

Sea horses eat all day long. One sea horse ate 50 times a day!

How many times did the sea horse eat in 3 days?

Work Space:

Answer:

_____ times

Daily Word Problems

WEEK 17 • DAY 3

Sea Horses

An aquarium has 43 yellow sea horses. It also has 55 gray sea horses.

How many sea horses are in the aquarium?

Work Space:

Answer:

_____ sea horses

Daily Word Problems

WEEK 17 • DAY 4

Sea Horses

Many sea horse eggs hatch in 45 days.

A sea horse laid its eggs 6 days ago. How many more days will it be until the eggs hatch?

Work Space:

Answer:

_____ days

Daily Word Problems

WEEK 17 • DAY 5

Sea Horses

People at one aquarium were studying sea horses. They put tags on the sea horses to keep track of them. Each tag had a 3-digit number.

Look at the tags on the sea horses. Write the numbers in order from the smallest to the largest.

smallest _____

_____

_____

_____

largest _____

Daily Word Problems

WEEK 18 • DAY 1

Balloons

The Balloon Man sells balloons. He started making balloon animals at 9:45. He stopped 1 hour later.

At what time did the Balloon Man stop?

Work Space:

Show your answer on the clock.

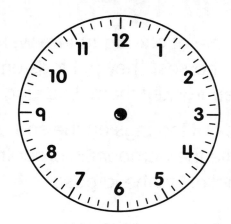

Answer:

_____ : _____

Daily Word Problems

WEEK 18 • DAY 2

Balloons

On Friday the Balloon Man sold 54 balloons. On Saturday he sold 70 balloons.

How many more balloons did he sell on Saturday than on Friday?

Work Space:

Answer:

_____ more

Daily Word Problems

WEEK 18 • DAY 3

Balloons

The Balloon Man had 25 dog balloons, 32 monkey balloons, and 14 rabbit balloons.

How many balloons did the Balloon Man have?

Work Space:

Answer:

_____ balloons

Daily Word Problems

WEEK 18 • DAY 4

Balloons

Eli bought some balloons. He paid with a dollar bill and 2 quarters.

How much did the balloons cost?

Work Space:

Answer:

$_____

Daily Word Problems

Balloons

The Balloon Man made a sign for his best-selling balloons.

Balloons for Sale

Star Balloon	$1.00
Heart Balloon	$2.00
Tiger Balloon	$3.00

1. How much would 1 heart balloon and 1 tiger balloon cost?

   $_____

2. How much would 3 star balloons and 2 heart balloons cost?

   $_____

3. Yumi bought 3 balloons. She spent $9.00. What did she buy?

   _____

Daily Word Problems

WEEK 19 • DAY 1

On the Farm

Farmer Mac has apple trees on his farm. They grow in 3 rows. There are 5 trees in each row.

How many apple trees does Farmer Mac have?

Work Space:

Answer:

_____ apple trees

Daily Word Problems

WEEK 19 • DAY 2

On the Farm

Gertie the hen lays 5 eggs a week. So far this year, she has laid 200 eggs!

In 4 more weeks, how many eggs in all will Gertie have laid?

Work Space:

Start at 200. Count by fives to solve the problem. Fill in the missing numbers.

200, _____, _____,

_____, _____

Answer:

_____ eggs

Daily Word Problems

WEEK 19 • DAY 3

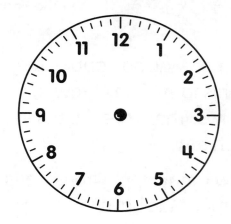

On the Farm

Sonia helps milk the cows. It takes her 15 minutes to milk each cow. She has to milk 3 cows. She starts at 6:00.

At what time will Sonia finish milking the cows?

Work Space:

Show your answer on the clock.

Answer:

_____ : _____

Daily Word Problems

WEEK 19 • DAY 4

On the Farm

Farmer Mac has a garden that is shaped like a rectangle. He is going to divide it in half. He will plant flowers in one half and vegetables in the other half.

How many different ways can the garden be divided?

Work Space:

Draw a rectangle for each different way. Draw a line on each to show how it is divided in half.

Answer:

_____ different ways

Daily Word Problems

WEEK 19 • DAY 5

On the Farm

Look at the map. It shows how far away
Farmer Mac's animals are from one another.

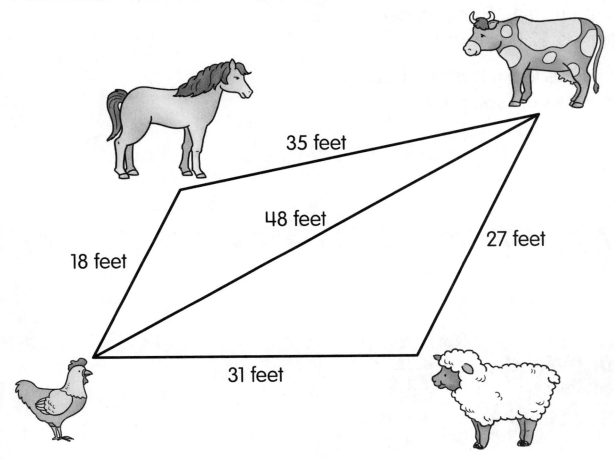

35 feet

48 feet

18 feet

27 feet

31 feet

1. How long is the path from the hen
   to the sheep to the cow?   _____ feet

2. How long is the path from the cow
   to the horse to the hen?   _____ feet

3. How long is the path from the horse
   to the hen to the cow?   _____ feet

Daily Word Problems

WEEK 20 • DAY 1

Apples

There was a sign by the apple farm. It said, "Pick your own apples. $2.00 a basket."

If you picked 4 baskets, how much would you pay?

Work Space:

Answer:

$ _____

Daily Word Problems

Apples

WEEK 20 • DAY 2

Teo and Lisa went apple picking. Teo picked 21 apples. Lisa picked 6 fewer apples.

1. How many apples did Lisa pick?

2. How many apples did the children pick in all?

Work Space:

Answer:

1. _____ apples

2. _____ apples in all

Daily Word Problems • EMC 7112 • © Evan-Moor Corp.

Daily Word Problems

WEEK 20 • DAY 3

Apples

A store had apples for sale. There were 150 red apples. There were 100 green apples.

How many apples were for sale?

Work Space:

Answer:

_____ apples

Daily Word Problems

WEEK 20 • DAY 4

Apples

It takes 9 apples to make an apple pie. Ethan has 20 apples.

1. How many apple pies can Ethan make?

2. If Ethan makes the pies, how many apples will he have left?

Work Space:

Answer:

1. _____ apple pies

2. _____ apples left

Daily Word Problems

WEEK 20 • DAY 5

Apples

Azad, Luke, and Cami each made an apple pie.

- Azad cut his pie in half.
- Luke cut his pie into thirds.
- Cami cut her pie into fourths.

Draw lines to show how the pies were cut.

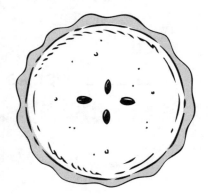

Azad's pie

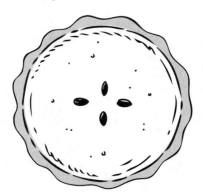

Luke's pie

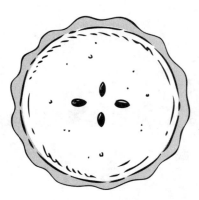

Cami's pie

1. How many equal parts did Azad's pie have? _____ parts

2. How many equal parts did Luke's pie have? _____ parts

3. How many equal parts did Cami's pie have? _____ parts

Daily Word Problems

WEEK 21 • DAY 1

Nifty Nut Shop

The Nifty Nut Shop sells bags of mixed nuts. Each bag is filled with 40 peanuts, 25 almonds, 15 walnuts, and 15 pecans.

How many nuts are in one bag?

Work Space:

Answer:

_____ nuts

Daily Word Problems

WEEK 21 • DAY 2

Nifty Nut Shop

Chen and Tran bought bags of peanuts. Chen's bag had 201 peanuts. Tran's bag had 210 peanuts.

1. Who had more peanuts?

2. How many more peanuts did he have?

Work Space:

Answer:

1. _____

2. _____ more peanuts

Daily Word Problems

WEEK 21 • DAY 3

Nifty Nut Shop

A small bag of almonds costs $2.00. A large bag of almonds costs $5.00. Mrs. Lopez wants to buy 2 small bags and 2 large bags.

How much money will she pay?

Work Space:

Answer:

$_____

Daily Word Problems

WEEK 21 • DAY 4

Nifty Nut Shop

It is 5:45. The Nifty Nut Shop will close in 15 minutes.

At what time will the shop close?

Work Space:

Show your answer on the clock.

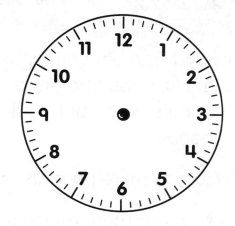

Answer:

_____ : _____

Daily Word Problems

WEEK 21 • DAY 5

Nifty Nut Shop

The graph shows how many bags of nuts the Nifty Nut Shop sold today.

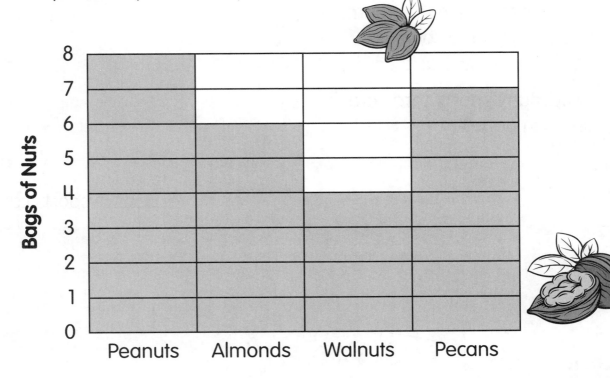

1. How many more bags of peanuts were sold than bags of almonds?

   _____ more bags

2. How many fewer bags of walnuts were sold than bags of pecans?

   _____ fewer bags

3. How many bags were sold in all?

   _____ bags

Daily Word Problems

WEEK 22 • DAY 1

Collections

Max collects sports cards. He keeps them in an album. Each page has 3 rows of cards. Each row has 3 cards.

How many sports cards are on each page?

Work Space:

Answer:

_____ sports cards

Daily Word Problems

WEEK 22 • DAY 2

Collections

Shayna collects bears. She has 32 stuffed bears and 19 glass bears. She also has 14 bears made from wood.

How many bears does Shayna have in all?

Work Space:

Answer:

_____ bears

Daily Word Problems • EMC 7112 • © Evan-Moor Corp.

Daily Word Problems

Collections

Three friends collect comic books. Simon has 65 comic books. Kara has 10 more books than Simon. Tyrone has 10 more books than Kara.

How many comic books does Tyrone have?

Work Space:

Answer:

_____ comic books

Daily Word Problems

Collections

Leah and Micah both collect stamps. Leah has 200 stamps. Micah has 235 stamps.

How many more stamps does Micah have than Leah?

Work Space:

Answer:

_____ more

Daily Word Problems

Collections

The Turner triplets collect stickers.

- Tammi gets 5 new stickers each week.
- Tony gets 10 new stickers each week.
- Toby gets 2 new stickers each week.

Skip-count to find out how many stickers each child has after 3 more weeks. Fill in the missing numbers.

Tammi   200, 205, _____, _____, _____

Tony   240, 250, _____, _____, _____

Toby   280, 282, _____, _____, _____

In 3 more weeks, who will have the most stickers? _____

Daily Word Problems

WEEK 23 • DAY 1

In the Kitchen

Naomi uses 3 oranges to make 1 cup of orange juice. She wants to make 5 cups of juice.

How many oranges does Naomi need?

Work Space:

Answer:

_____ oranges

Daily Word Problems

WEEK 23 • DAY 2

In the Kitchen

Curtis is making muffins. The recipe makes 24 muffins.

If Curtis doubles the recipe, how many muffins will he make?

Work Space:

Answer:

_____ muffins

Daily Word Problems

WEEK 23 • DAY 3

In the Kitchen

Emma made 3 large cookies. She used icing to write these numbers on them:

 7 4 9

What is the largest number she can make? What is the smallest?

Work Space:

Answer:

largest number _____

smallest number _____

Daily Word Problems

WEEK 23 • DAY 4

In the Kitchen

The clock shows when Lori put a cake in the oven.

1. At what time did Lori put the cake in?

2. The cake will be done in 1 hour. At what time will it be done?

Work Space:

Answer:

1. _____ : _____

2. _____ : _____

Daily Word Problems

In the Kitchen

Nadia and Burt made a pizza. They divided the pizza into fourths. Then they put 5 slices of pepperoni on each fourth.

Draw lines to show how the pizza was divided.

Then draw small circles to show the pepperoni slices on each fourth.

1. How many equal parts did the pizza have? _____ parts

2. How many slices of pepperoni were on the pizza? _____ slices

Daily Word Problems

WEEK 24 • DAY 1

Happy Birthday

Jason and Jenny are twins. It will be their birthday on the 27th day of the month.

If today is the 9th day of the month, how many more days is it until the twins' birthday?

Work Space:

Answer:

_____ more days

Daily Word Problems

WEEK 24 • DAY 2

Happy Birthday

Romi put candles on her grandma's birthday cake. She used one candle for each year old. She used 16 pink candles, 18 blue ones, 14 green ones, and 15 yellow ones.

How old is Romi's grandma?

Work Space:

Answer:

_____ years old

Daily Word Problems

WEEK 24 • DAY 3

Happy Birthday

Great-Grandpa had a huge cake at his birthday party. The cake was cut into 120 pieces. One hundred people each got a piece.

How many pieces of cake were left?

Work Space:

Answer:

_____ pieces

Daily Word Problems

Happy Birthday

WEEK 24 • DAY 4

It was Abdul's birthday. He got 6 five-dollar bills from his uncle.

How much money did Abdul get from his uncle?

Work Space:

Answer:

$_____

Daily Word Problems

Happy Birthday

Everyone in Kimi's family has a birthday in the first four months of the year.

Birthdays

Mom – February 4
Dad – January 8
Kimi – April 17
Jon – January 21
Grandma – January 26
Grandpa – April 9
Uncle Dan – January 30
Auntie Val – February 20
Kelli – April 27
Josh – March 5
Ben – April 13
Taylor – January 17

Make tally marks to count how many birthdays are in each month.

January _____   March _____

February _____   April _____

1. Which month has the most birthdays?   _____

2. How many birthdays are in that month?   _____ birthdays

Daily Word Problems

WEEK 25 • DAY 1

Art Class

Mrs. Evans is an art teacher. She has 63 students in first grade, 85 students in second grade, and 72 students in third grade.

How many students does Mrs. Evans teach?

Work Space:

Answer:

_____ students

Daily Word Problems

WEEK 25 • DAY 2

Art Class

Wanda looked at her watch. She said, "I'd better hurry. Art class starts in 10 minutes!" Here is what she saw:

At what time does her class start?

Work Space:

Show your answer on the clock.

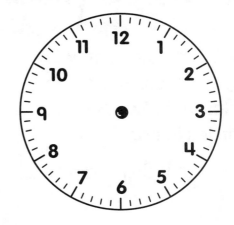

Answer:

_____ : _____

Daily Word Problems

WEEK 25 • DAY 3

Art Class

Darien drew a rectangle to make a flag. He divided the shape into thirds. He colored each part of the flag in a different color.

How many colors did he use?

Work Space:

Draw lines on the rectangle to show how Darien may have divided the shape.

Answer:

_____ colors

Daily Word Problems

WEEK 25 • DAY 4

Art Class

Yuki made a design with paper circles. She put the circles in 3 rows. She put 5 circles in each row.

How many circles did Yuki use?

Work Space:

Answer:

_____ circles

Daily Word Problems

Art Class

Mrs. Cook's students put on an art show.
The chart shows what the students painted.

Picture	Number of Paintings
People	81
Animals	42
Flowers	69
Toys	28

1. What did most students paint
   a picture of?   _____

2. How many more students painted
   flowers than animals?   _____ more

3. How many more students painted
   people than toys?   _____ more

Daily Word Problems

Gizmo Robot

Gizmo is a robot. He likes to help in the kitchen. Do you need to open a can of soup? Ask Gizmo. He can open 36 cans in 1 minute!

How many cans would Gizmo be able to open in 3 minutes?

Work Space:

Answer:

_____ cans

Daily Word Problems

Gizmo Robot

Gizmo was dusting the living room and found some money. He found 1 dollar bill, 1 quarter, 5 nickels, and 3 pennies.

How much money did Gizmo find?

Work Space:

Answer:

$_____

Daily Word Problems

WEEK 26 • DAY 3

Gizmo Robot

Gizmo is very strong. Yesterday he lifted a sofa so he could clean under it. Ruff the dog was sitting on the sofa, too!

The sofa was 300 pounds and Ruff was 45 pounds. How much did they weigh together?

Work Space:

Answer:

_____ pounds

Daily Word Problems

WEEK 26 • DAY 4

Gizmo Robot

Gizmo can read fast. On Monday he read a book with 600 pages. On Tuesday he read a book with 800 pages.

How many more pages did Gizmo read on Tuesday than on Monday?

Work Space:

Answer:

_____ more pages

Daily Word Problems

WEEK 26 • DAY 5

Gizmo is always fixing things. Today he is going to fix some clocks that are missing their minute hand. Can you help?

Look at each clock. Draw the minute hand to match each time.

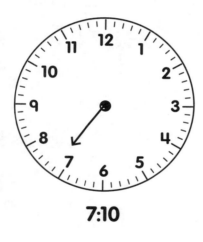

7:10

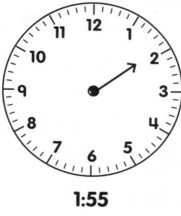

1:55

9:40

11:05

3:50

12:20

Daily Word Problems

WEEK 27 • DAY 1

Play Ball!

There were 123 girls and 105 boys playing with a ball at recess.

How many students were playing with a ball?

Work Space:

Answer:

_____ students

Daily Word Problems

WEEK 27 • DAY 2

Play Ball!

Aaron's school has 70 rubber balls. This year each second-grade classroom got 2 new balls. There are 4 second-grade classrooms.

How many rubber balls does the school have now?

Work Space:

Count by twos to solve the problem.

70, _____, _____, _____,

_____

Answer:

_____ balls

Daily Word Problems

WEEK 27 • DAY 3

Play Ball!

Kacee bought a soccer ball. It cost $8.00. Kacee gave the store clerk 2 five-dollar bills.

How much change did Kacee get back?

Work Space:

Answer:

$_____

Daily Word Problems

WEEK 27 • DAY 4

Play Ball!

Jordan's basketball team plays two games every week. Last week the team scored a total of 102 points. This week the team scored a total of 116 points.

How many more points did the team score this week?

Work Space:

Answer:

_____ more points

Daily Word Problems

WEEK 27 • DAY 5

Play Ball!

A sports store kept track of how many balls were sold last week.

Balls Sold Last Week

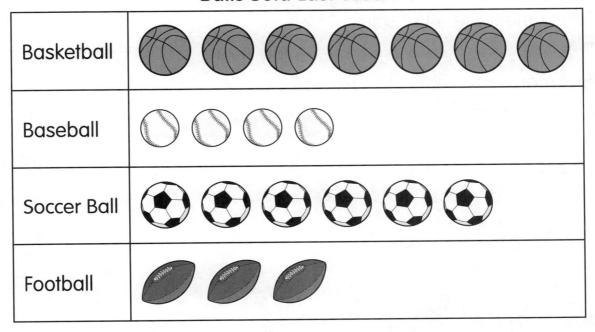

1. Which ball did the most people buy? _____

2. Which ball did the least number of people buy? _____

3. How many balls were sold altogether? _____ balls

Daily Word Problems

WEEK 28 • DAY 1

Crawly Critters

Seth and Jake saw a line of ants on the sidewalk. "There must be 320 ants!" said Seth. "I think there are 645," said Jake.

How many more ants did Jake guess than Seth?

Work Space:

Answer:

_____ more

Daily Word Problems

WEEK 28 • DAY 2

Crawly Critters

Jess went on a bug hunt. She counted 12 caterpillars, 35 ants, 29 ladybugs, and 8 crickets.

How many bugs did she see in all?

Work Space:

Answer:

_____ bugs

Daily Word Problems

WEEK 28 • DAY 3

Crawly Critters

Alma saw a spider catch a fly in its web. Suppose a spider ate 10 flies a day.

1. How many flies would it eat in 1 week?

2. How many days would it take the spider to eat 100 flies?

Work Space:

Answer:

1. _____ flies

2. _____ days

Daily Word Problems

WEEK 28 • DAY 4

Crawly Critters

A centipede looks like a worm with many legs. Some centipedes have 170 pairs of legs!

There are 2 legs in every pair. How many legs are in 170 pairs?

Work Space:

Answer:

_____ legs

Daily Word Problems

WEEK 28 • DAY 5

Crawly Critters

One night Kerri, Teri, and Jerry caught fireflies in jars. Kerri caught 24 fireflies. Teri caught half as many as Kerri. Jerry caught half as many as Teri.

1. How many fireflies did Teri catch?

_____ fireflies

2. How many fireflies did Jerry catch?

_____ fireflies

3. How many fireflies did the children catch altogether?

_____ fireflies

Daily Word Problems

WEEK 29 • DAY 1

In the Garden

Kanisha is watering her flower garden. The flowers are planted in 5 rows. Each row has 5 flowers.

How many flowers are in Kanisha's garden?

Work Space:

Answer:

_____ flowers

Daily Word Problems

WEEK 29 • DAY 2

In the Garden

Elena bought a packet of bean seeds and a packet of tomato seeds. She paid with 2 one-dollar bills, 3 dimes, and 2 nickels.

How much did the two packets of seeds cost?

Work Space:

Answer:

$_____

Daily Word Problems

WEEK 29 • DAY 3

In the Garden

Mr. Green has some rose bushes. He counted 125 red roses and 108 yellow roses.

How many more red roses does he have than yellow roses?

Work Space:

Answer:

_____ more red roses

Daily Word Problems

WEEK 29 • DAY 4

In the Garden

It took 20 minutes for a snail to get across a garden. The clock shows when it started.

1. At what time did the snail start?

2. At what time did it get to the other side?

Work Space:

Answer:

1. _____ : _____

2. _____ : _____

Daily Word Problems

WEEK 29 • DAY 5

In the Garden

There were 65 bees in the garden at 4:00 p.m. One hour later, 10 bees left. Every hour after that, 10 bees left the garden. Fill in the chart to show how many bees were left in the garden each hour.

Time	4:00	5:00	6:00	7:00	8:00
Number of Bees	65	55			

1. How many bees were in the garden at 7:00 p.m.?   _____ bees

2. How many bees were in the garden at 8:00 p.m.?   _____ bees

3. How many fewer bees were in the garden at 8:00 than at 4:00?   _____ fewer bees

Daily Word Problems

WEEK 30 • DAY 1

Caterpillars

A butterfly farm had 440 butterfly eggs. When they hatched, a caterpillar came out of each one.

If 260 of the caterpillars were green, how many were a different color?

Work Space:

Answer:

_____ caterpillars

Daily Word Problems

WEEK 30 • DAY 2

Caterpillars

A caterpillar keeps eating and growing. It stops when it reaches its full size. At the butterfly farm, this takes 14 days.

A caterpillar hatched on May 16. On what day will it reach its full size?

Work Space:

Answer:

_____

Daily Word Problems

WEEK 30 • DAY 3

Caterpillars

The hickory horned devil caterpillar is really big. It is about 14 centimeters long. That is as long as a hot dog!

If you lined up 3 of these caterpillars from end to end, how long would the line be?

Work Space:

Answer:

_____ centimeters

Daily Word Problems

WEEK 30 • DAY 4

Caterpillars

One caterpillar may eat 175 leaves before it turns into a butterfly.

How many leaves would 2 caterpillars eat?

Work Space:

Answer:

_____ leaves

Daily Word Problems

Caterpillars

Tyson and Tara counted caterpillars in four different parts of the forest. Here is what they found out:

Area A	408 caterpillars
Area B	157 caterpillars
Area C	713 caterpillars
Area D	326 caterpillars

1. Write the numbers in order from the least to the greatest.

   —————, —————, —————, —————

2. Find the area that had the greatest number of caterpillars. How many more did it have than the area with the fewest caterpillars?

   ——————— more caterpillars

Daily Word Problems

WEEK 31 • DAY 1

Let's Bike!

There are 384 students at Tamara's school. Most of them have bikes.

If 319 students have bikes, how many do **not** have bikes?

Work Space:

Answer:

_____ students

Daily Word Problems

WEEK 31 • DAY 2

Let's Bike!

At Miguel's school, there are 49 students who ride their bikes to school on Fridays. There are also 136 students who ride their bikes to school every day.

How many bikes are at the school on Fridays?

Work Space:

Answer:

_____ bikes

Daily Word Problems

WEEK 31 • DAY 3

Let's Bike!

Alina and her family go biking every weekend. They ride a total of 10 miles each time. So far this year, they have biked 200 miles.

How many miles will they have biked after 6 more weekends?

Work Space:

Count by 10 to solve the problem. Fill in the missing numbers.

200, _____, _____, _____,

_____, _____, _____

Answer:

_____ miles

Daily Word Problems

WEEK 31 • DAY 4

Let's Bike!

Some people were riding their bikes at the park in the morning. Fourteen left at noon. Then 28 people were left biking at the park.

How many people were biking at the park in the morning?

Work Space:

Answer:

_____ people

Daily Word Problems

WEEK 31 • DAY 5

Let's Bike!

The chart shows the different colors of bikes at a school.

Bike Colors

Orange	~~||||~~ ~~||||~~ ||||
Green	~~||||~~ ~~||||~~ ~~||||~~ ~~||||~~ ~~||||~~ ~~||||~~
Red	~~||||~~ ~~||||~~ ~~||||~~ ~~||||~~ ~~||||~~ ||
Blue	~~||||~~ ~~||||~~ ~~||||~~ ~~||||~~ ~~||||~~ ~~||||~~ ~~||||~~ ~~||||~~	

1. How many more blue bikes were there than orange bikes? _____ more

2. How many more green bikes were there than red bikes? _____ more

3. How many bikes were there in all? _____ bikes

Daily Word Problems

WEEK 32 • DAY 1

At the Library

The library just got some new books. There are 73 books for children and 89 books for adults.

How many new books did the library get?

Work Space:

Answer:

_____ books

Daily Word Problems

WEEK 32 • DAY 2

At the Library

Storytime is every Friday morning. The clock shows when it starts. Storytime lasts for 1 hour.

1. At what time does it start?

2. At what time does it end?

Work Space:

Answer:

1. _____ : _____

2. _____ : _____

Daily Word Problems • EMC 7112 • © Evan-Moor Corp.

Daily Word Problems

WEEK 32 • DAY 3

At the Library

The library hosted a puppet show. There were 120 people who went to see it. Forty-five were parents and the rest were children.

How many children went to the puppet show?

Work Space:

Answer:

_____ children

Daily Word Problems

At the Library

WEEK 32 • DAY 4

There will be a used book sale at the library next week. Children's books will cost 50¢ each.

If you had 2 one-dollar bills, how many children's books could you buy?

Work Space:

Answer:

_____ books

Daily Word Problems

WEEK 32 • DAY 5

At the Library

The Joytown Library has lots of dinosaur books. How many does it have? Use the clues to find out.

Clues

- The number is between 300 and 400.
- You say the number when you count by twos.
- You say the number when you count by fives.
- You say the number when you count by tens.
- The digits in the number add up to 10.

1. How many dinosaur books can you find at Joytown Library?

_____ books

2. Write another clue about the number you found.

_____

_____

_____

Daily Word Problems

WEEK 33 • DAY 1

On Vacation

Maya's family is going on a plane trip. The flight will leave at 2:50 in the afternoon. The family has to be at the airport 2 hours before their flight.

At what time should Maya's family arrive at the airport?

Work Space:

Show your answer on the clock.

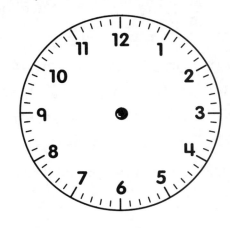

Answer:

_____ : _____

Daily Word Problems

WEEK 33 • DAY 2

On Vacation

The Simpsons went to a science museum. There were 750 visitors at the museum.

If 425 of the visitors were children, how many were adults?

Work Space:

Answer:

_____ adults

Daily Word Problems

WEEK 33 • DAY 3

On Vacation

Jeremy and his family drove to a lake. They drove 102 miles from home and stopped for lunch. They still needed to drive 89 miles to get to the lake.

How far was the lake from Jeremy's home?

Work Space:

Answer:

_____ miles

Daily Word Problems

WEEK 33 • DAY 4

On Vacation

Kruti and her family went to an amusement park. Kruti liked the Space Ride the best. She saw 28 red space aliens, 32 blue ones, and 4 silver ones.

How many space aliens did Kruti see on the ride?

Work Space:

Answer:

_____ space aliens

Daily Word Problems

WEEK 33 · DAY 5

On Vacation

Look at the map. The numbers show how many miles were traveled.

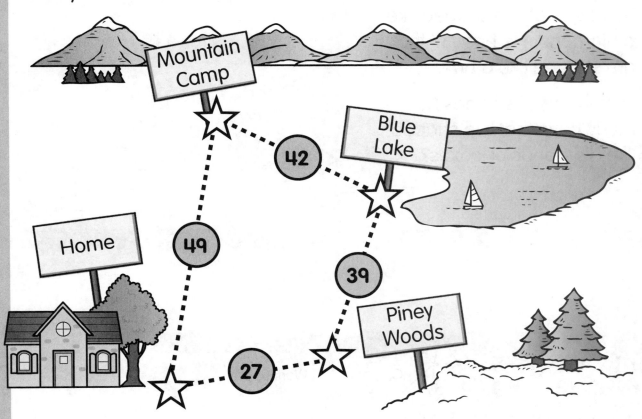

1. The Hays drove from home to Piney Woods. They stopped for lunch and then drove to Blue Lake for a swim. Then they drove to Mountain Camp. How many miles did they travel? _____ miles

2. After a few days, the Hays drove from Mountain Camp back to their home. They took the fastest way. How many miles did they travel? _____ miles

3. How many fewer miles did they travel going home than going to Mountain Camp? _____ fewer miles

Daily Word Problems

WEEK 34 • DAY 1

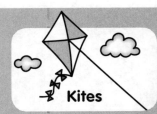
Kites

Mr. McFly sells kites. He has 126 that are shaped like a diamond. He has 137 that are shaped like a box.

How many kites does Mr. McFly have that are shaped like diamonds or boxes?

Work Space:

Answer:

_____ kites

Daily Word Problems

WEEK 34 • DAY 2

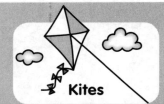
Kites

Mr. McFly has 150 kites that are shaped like butterflies or bats.

If he has 85 butterfly kites, how many bat kites does he have?

Work Space:

Answer:

_____ bat kites

Daily Word Problems

WEEK 34 • DAY 3

Kites

Janey wants to buy a kite. It costs $15.00.

What bills can Janey use to pay for the kite? How many will she need of each kind of bill?

Work Space:

Draw the bills here.

Answer:

_____

_____

Daily Word Problems

WEEK 34 • DAY 4

Kites

Hannah started flying her kite at 3:35. She flew the kite for 20 minutes.

At what time did Hannah stop flying her kite?

Work Space:

Show your answer on the clock.

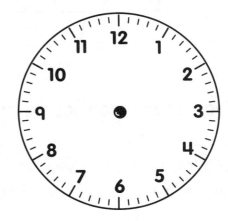

Answer:

_____ : _____

Daily Word Problems

WEEK 34 • DAY 5

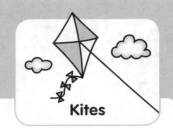

Kites

Some children were flying kites at a park.
The graph shows the different colors of the kites.
Each kite in the graph stands for 2 kites.

Kite Colors

Green	🪁
Yellow	🪁 🪁 🪁 🪁 🪁 🪁
Red	🪁 🪁 🪁 🪁
Purple	🪁 🪁

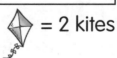 = 2 kites

1. How many red kites were there? _____ red kites

2. How many more yellow kites
   were there than green kites? _____ more

3. How many kites were at the park? _____ kites

Daily Word Problems

WEEK 35 • DAY 1

Safari Park

There were 457 visitors at Safari Park on Saturday. There were 486 visitors on Sunday.

How many visitors went to Safari Park on the weekend?

Work Space:

Answer:

_____ visitors

Daily Word Problems

WEEK 35 • DAY 2

Safari Park

Safari Park has 15 lions. It has 2 fewer tigers than lions. It has 4 more cheetahs than lions.

These animals are in the big cat area. How many big cats are at Safari Park?

Work Space:

Fill in the missing numbers to solve the problem.

_____ + _____ + _____ = _____

Answer:

_____ big cats

Daily Word Problems

WEEK 35 • DAY 3

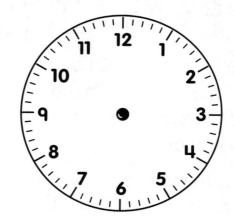

Safari Park

The animal keeper feeds the tigers at 2:15 in the afternoon. She feeds the giraffes 3 hours earlier.

At what time are the giraffes fed?

Work Space:

Show your answer on the clock.

Answer:

_____ : _____

Daily Word Problems

WEEK 35 • DAY 4

Safari Park

A baby elephant was born at Safari Park exactly 1 week ago. The baby weighed 250 pounds at birth. It has gained 2 pounds a day.

How much does the baby elephant weigh now?

Work Space:

Count by twos to solve the problem. Fill in the missing numbers.

250, _____, _____, _____,

_____, _____, _____,

_____

Answer:

_____ pounds

Safari Park

Carmen went to Safari Park's gift shop and bought a book about giraffes. She spent exactly this much money:

Circle the book that Carmen bought.

Giraffe Facts — $4.65

Giraffes and Their Babies — $4.90

Amazing Giraffes — $4.80

Daily Word Problems

WEEK 36 • DAY 1

Summer Fun

There were 128 boys and 153 girls at Slip and Dive Water Park.

1. How many children went to the water park?

2. How many more girls went than boys?

Work Space:

Answer:

1. _____ children

2. _____ more girls

Daily Word Problems

WEEK 36 • DAY 2

Summer Fun

Joy-Lin and Kei were at the beach looking for shells. Joy-Lin found 2 more than Kei did. Together they found 36 shells.

How many shells did each child find?

Work Space:

Answer:

Joy-Lin found _____ shells.

Kei found _____ shells.

Daily Word Problems

WEEK 36 • DAY 3

Summer Fun

Nine people went on a picnic. They shared 16 peanut butter cookies and 16 oatmeal cookies. Each person ate 2 cookies.

How many cookies were left?

Work Space:

Answer:

_____ cookies

Daily Word Problems

Summer Fun

WEEK 36 • DAY 4

Brett and his dad like to go hiking to look for birds. Last week they counted 125 birds. This week they counted 118 birds.

How many birds did they count in all?

Work Space:

Answer:

_____ birds

Daily Word Problems

Summer Fun

There were rowboat races on the lake all day.
The winning boats were shown on a chart.
The winner of each race won $10 and a ribbon.
At the end of the day, the winner of the most
races won an extra $20 and a trophy.

Rowboat Winners!

Rowboat A won 3 races.

Rowboat B won 6 races.

Rowboat C won 2 races.

Rowboat D won 4 races.

1. How many races took place? _____ races

2. Which boat won the most races? Rowboat _____

   How much money did the crew
   of that boat win? $_____

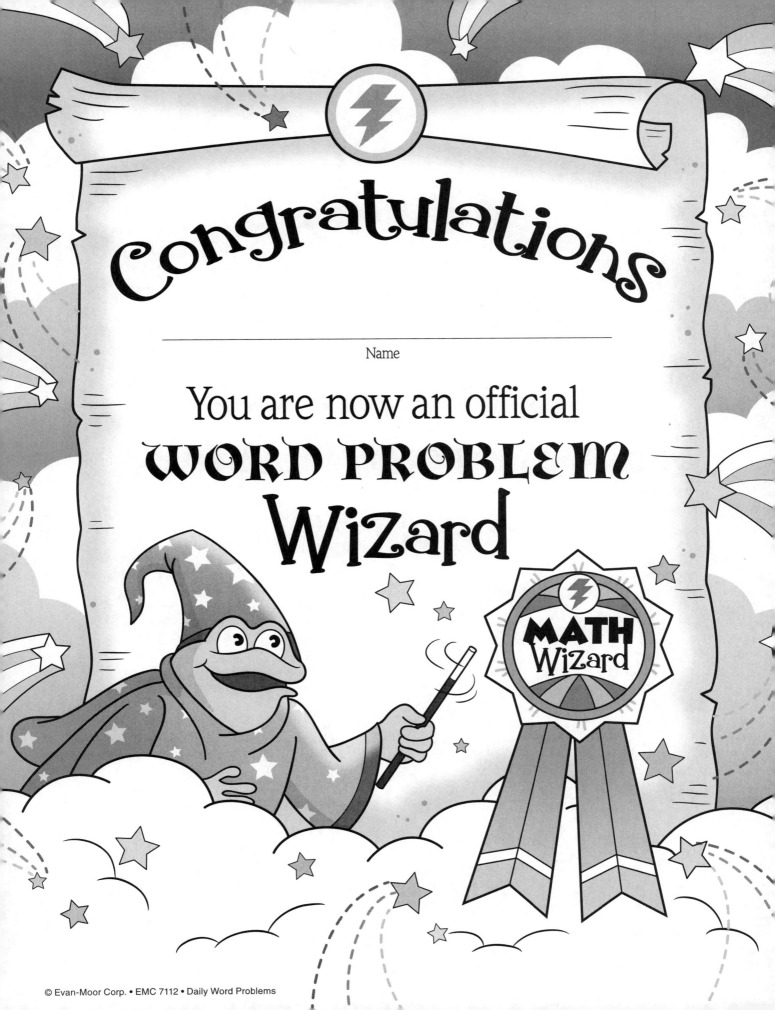

Congratulations

_____
Name

You are now an official
WORD PROBLEM
Wizard

MATH Wizard